Word Crumbs

A Poetry Collection

Jennifer Faye D'Amato

BookLeaf Publishing

India | USA | UK

Made with ❤ on the BookLeaf Publishing Platform
www.bookleafpub.in
www.bookleafpub.com

Dedication

I dedicate these pages to every woman who ever doubted
herself, lost track of her voice or could not find words to
describe her feelings. And especially to late bloomers,
like me, trying to expose their sassy.

Preface

I just forgot Annie Lamott's name for a second and then remembered it again. I try to channel her "butt in chair" guidance, but I know she'd forgive me for standing up to type. Like many my age, I fear that I will start to have memory issues and that if I don't write soon my chance will be gone. I've already waited until I am one month away from being 70. I've always loved writing and I am best known for my annual holiday letters, which I hope will live on as a sort of family journal. I was 8 when I wrote my first book, Biography of A Penny. Despite rave reviews locally (the living room), Ship Of Fools by Katherine Anne Porter took the #1 spot as best selling novel in 1962. I can't pinpoint the exact moment I put my words on a high shelf right next to my voice and didn't take them down again for many decades. So here I am, while memory serves, with my feelings and my voice excited to finally unite with words and join me. I hope to do them justice.

Acknowledgements

I would like to extend my infinite gratitude to women I have known and loved since childhood - my mother, Garnet Lillegard D'Amato Horton, grandmother Giovanna Rosa D'Amato, and grandmother Lela Faye Fatland Lillegard. I must mention my Italian aunts in their red lipstick and fingernails who sat at Uncle Jimmy's basement bar, and my Norwegian family ladies whose incredibly quick wit was delicious, like fresh ground coffee. To Mrs. Doctor, the first-grade teacher I crushed on so hard that I mimicked her overbite in my school photo that year. To Cathy Wendorf, the best friend I was fortunate to make during middle school when I most needed her to find me. To the mentors, colleagues, members of book clubs and neighborhoods, support groups, and casts - I continue to learn from you and delight in time spent with you. Thank you to my beloved family, especially those who call me mom, aunt, stepmom, in law and cousin. You make my world a loving place, and I am deeply honored to be in yours. I acknowledge, and can never thank enough, my husband Randy Cullen, for the love, support and encouragement he consistently and bravely offers my creative urges.

What Barbra Means To Me

Another email from Barbra today, October 11, 2024
Much apprehension about Pennsylvania
It will look vulgar in red she says, that trend cannot
spread
I will feel Guilty if I Rain on her Parade
I know that People who need People are the luckiest
She Touched Me forever by her Happy Days duet on the
Judy Garland show when I was 9
Belting, I could escape in the sound of my voice, IF I was
alone....maybe because I was alone
Like me, she'd grown herself a nose too large for her face
- but her confidence ignited my hidden, shy, Funny Girl
I credit Barbra for my inspiration, that's just The Way
We Were
I performed Evergreen at a friend's wedding, one of my
favorite college Memories
As life evolved I became a Woman In Love with many
additional music genres and performers
But for Barbra, my Love Will Survive.... so yes Babs, I
will send another $15 ... + tip

Middle School

Who was your best friend right before me?
How did she feel when kicked to the street?
Was there a hint about being replaced?
I can picture the questioning hurt on her face
I am so fortunate you chose me
And I love you more than ever
But I do wonder what might happen
if you find somebody better....

Parody: Longfellow's Hiawatha

The Song Of The Great Fox River (1971)

Should you ask, whence pollution
Whence the Fox, o'river great,
With odor of the sewer,
With the dew and damp of smog
With the curling smoke of factories,
With the heavy humid bog
I should answer, I should tell you
From the industry in thrown
Huge amounts of wasted substance
To be kicked and washed and blown
Through the parks once filled with beauty,
Travels trash, and garbage too,
Cluttering our once clean city.
By the shores of the Great Fox River,
By the slimy, mucky water
Stood the Council of the City,
Saying "No more is it pretty,
No more is there any beauty,
In the river of our city."

Many days they talked together,
Heeding all of wind and weather,
Questioned, listened, waited, answered,
Finally an answer came.
Ye who love the haunts of nature,
Love the sunshine of the meadow,
Love the shadow of the forest,
Love the wind among the branches,
Love the free and rambling land,
Unite together, join the cause,
Against pollution take your stand.
So the great rebirth began
Fresh new lakes and cleaner old,
Highways empty of all litter,
Rivers clean and running cold.
And our city, once disaster,
With the smog in one huge cloud,
Now stands with its Great Fox River,
Brave and clean and proud

My Own White Flag

I surrendered a chance to dance the lead in our grade
school ballet recital because I refused to let a boy pick
me up and spin me around.
Later, I surrendered the chance to play Shirley Temple in
a Sunday School play - I had the hair for it but not the
nerve.
I surrendered tennis almost immediately because I wasn't
coordinated enough on day one
I surrendered being in the chorus of the community
theater play because I had been hoping for a lead part
I surrendered trying to make friends in my new middle
school because I was quiet, depressed, and excessively
sweaty
I surrendered singing in the shower because my sister
craved my father's attentive vocal coaching and I did not
Apparently my parents never taught me that trying is
enough, that everyone needs practice, that I need to
show myself compassion while I'm learning
I recall sitting in the curve of our tweed 1950's sectional
davenport wearing an intentionally pathetic, pouty
expression -
no one noticed. Is this one of the moments I learned that
my feelings do not matter?
Did I ever ignore my own daughter's bid for curiosity

about her own emotional experiences?

My mother was adored for her seemingly endless patience, her self-sacrificing, sweet, forgiving temperament.

But I saw the subtle clench in her jaw that I now feel in mine

Phased

Raised

Teenaged

Staged

Caged

Engaged

Praised

Maged

Trained

Played

Stayed

Dazed

Afraid

Caved

Crazed

Aged

Enraged

Drained

Blamed

Prayed

Faced

Waged

Bailed

Restaged

Reclaimed
Renamed
Braved
Raved
Waved

Touchstones

Taste:

Cotton candy at the Fair

Little yellow squares of Goldrush gum

Medjool Dates

Mom's Sunday spaghetti and chicken

Midwest Airlines' warm chocolate chip cookies

Caramels

Grandma Faye's Warm lefse

Popcorn....obviously

Touch:

Old fur shawl Aunt Isabel gave me when I was 6

My little cousin's marshmallow forehead

Infant toes

A scratch on the bullseye of an itch

My feet buried in sand

Holding his clean shaven face

Greasy popcorn fingertips ....obviously

Smell:

Leaves crunching on an October sidewalk

A perfume I wore in 1980, wish I could recall the name
Freshly ground A&P 8 o'clock coffee
My skin after being outside
His intoxicating neck on date night
Gasoline, (I just can't help it)
Popcorn...obviously

Sound:
Soundtracks to musicals
Infinite waves like puppy tongues
Grade school playgrounds during recess
Light rain as I go to sleep
Toddler giggles
Purring cat reverberating on my tummy
Popcorn....obviously

Sight:
The view from a Norwegian mountain
My babies sleeping and safe
Family videos of Christmas mornings
The bus from O'Hare arriving
A clean kitchen floor
Adult kids driving into the driveway
Lying on the grass and looking up at white fluffy clouds
Mesmerizing flames
Bowl of fresh popcorn.....

Oh, How I Must Love Thee

So much can annoy me, let me count the ways
It wouldn't pay to tell you, it is my nature to appease
But let us start with the obvious, your hundred decibel
sneeze
You say it can't be softer and I understand that, dear
It's just that to hear you summon me, it's best to have
good ears

Your teeth against your fork sends shock waves through
my head
The hearing aids I use I bought to lead the way for you
You did not end up getting yours, so what am I to do?
Your hankies look like dusting rags but you don't seem
to care
Perhaps you are distracted by that 5" eyebrow hair

'Round the house you'll wield a mop if I ask you to
I love that you'll cook dinner with never a complaint

The garlic lingers long my love, and not just on the plate
The trash pick up is Monday, don't ask me if I'm sure
When you coach me how to drive, the road becomes a
blur

From break of dawn 'til bedtime, you talk to our two
dogs
Occasionally you'll ask me, maybe twice, if I heard you
But I haven't paid attention so I haven't got a clue
The pups sure love you, sweetheart, I know I can't
compete
They know they can't rely on me for a blend of gourmet
treats

But alas, you listen to me when I need to vent or cry
You have ceased trying to fix my problems or my issues
You validate my feelings, or just hand me a tissue
We've had our share of struggles, and we often don't
agree
But you are still my person and forever you will be

Fall Walk

Like a lover, the breeze holds my face with both hands
and I look up, trusting, enamored
Sunshine tries to peek through dark glasses at my naked
eyes
Music massages my ears, a secret soundtrack to my soul
Is it obvious to those passing
that this stroll is really a dance?
My dog knows I am a child again
as I shimmy into the black rubber swing at the park
It squeezes my butt cheeks together and points my legs
askew
just as it did my mother when as an old woman she
loved to swing
Suddenly, I regret that we referred to her as "cute"
Nothing seems as settled as I expected at this senior age,
Not every mother is blessed with children equipped to
take flight
Regardless, gratitude is sorrow's antidote
And I return to the ordinary administration of my life,
renewed

Imperfectly Clear

Seems clearcut, complete clear headedness? unclear
Let us be clear, clear of worries, clear of stress,
Clear of memories, clearly a nightmare
Clear path obvious? clear the way!
The check won't clear, free or clear
Clear from suspicion, clear from debt
Clear my in basket, the fog will clear
Clear the dishes, clear the table
Clear your throat, speak clearly
Clear of guilt, clear conscience
those with clearance clear a room,
Clear winner, clearly unlikely
In the clearing, crystal clear

Contradictions

I can do anything
but cannot get myself going
I love humankind
but dislike so many people
I look forward to going out
but socializing exhausts me
I savor time alone
but can't be trusted with a quart of ice cream
My husband drives me crazy,
but I am crazy about him
I can stay in pajamas all day
but I adore dressing up
I'm honored to be aging,
but terrified of losing control

Retirement Goals Day 1

(How Did I Have Time to Work for Someone Else?)

Each Day:

Sleep 8 hours needed to regenerate the brain
Dress, Hair, Make Up 30"
Eat meals 60"
Exercise 45"
Drink 8 glasses of water 20"
Connect with husband 60"
Kegels 15"
Brain games 25"
Face yoga 20"
Tapping 15"
Save recipes on my phone 75"
Meditating 30"
Neuroplasticity exercises 15"
Healthy Food Plan, Buy Prep 90"
Fresh air 20"
TED Talk 20"
Connect with friends 30"

Play with the dogs 30"

Catch up with kids 60" (might include sending them
Instagrams they don't want)

Read the news 20"

Rest or nap   30"

Laugh Heartily 15"

Watch an episode of a series 60"

Ping Pong 20"

Check email, respond to texts 45"

Keep a journal 30"

Take supplements or have a smoothie 15"

Positive Affirmations 15"

Shower, bathroom 30"

Declutter 15"

Read a novel 45"

Online or in person class 60"

Music 20"

Straighten house and clean one room 30"

In Addition as Needed:

Look up household hacks

Write birthday gifts

Volunteer

Learn a new craft

Deep Condition Hair

Reconcile budget

Manicure and pedicure

Donate clothes

Plan the next vacation

Think of a gift for my husband - so hard

Preventive health appointments

Remove outdated items from fridge (before kids visit)

Pay bills

Clean out email

Update Passwords

Clean out the toaster tray

Vinegar the kettle

Clean out the drains

Dust ceiling fans

Shampoo rugs

Depression

Imagine a deep well, with sand at the bottom
I am standing in the sand looking up
To catch just a glimpse of light on my face
Before I lie down and curl up once again
To surrender to sleep and resume dreaming

Occasionally I wedge myself between the sides of the
well
and try to inch my way up
but almost immediately I fall back down
deciding its just easier to stay down here on the bottom
It's not so bad, less to explain, no expectations

I am incredibly heavy, my lungs at capacity with
hardening cement
My neck is twisted and my limbs succumb to gravity
My family peers down regularly and asks me how I am
I assure them I am ok and encourage them to enjoy the
day
I can't help them any longer.... but that's not the problem

I feel exhausted, too spent to rally, too weak to fight
My body tells me to take a break, pull over at a rest stop
and shut my eyes

I feel apologetic, guilty, ashamed
Is acceptance the same as giving up, I need to know
One seems practical, the latter like failing

Welcome, Future Me

Come in, come join me,
I say, waving to the most comfortable chair in the room
I am so intrigued to meet you
Tell me, would you like tea?
    Just water - you never drank enough water you know
I want to hear all about the family, but first, how are
you?
I see you are stooping over - just a bit, no offence
intended!
You wear mother's handed down hands
Did you ever have that second hip replaced?
You seem less stressed, have you practiced letting go,
finally?
So curious, what have you learned about yourself over
the last few years?
How so is life easier?
Or more challenging?
 I was sorry to hear about your friend, I know how close
                                        you were.
        Grief comes frequently, even expected over time -
                        relentlessly unavoidable
Did that IBS get under control I hope? Did having to shit
in the woods ever actually happen?

I don't think I told you often enough how proud I was of
you. I was often critical and expected too much. I see
how hard you're trying to feel the joy each day.
I know you do your best, I believe the kids know it too.
You did make an impact, not just a mess.
Please be kind with yourself, shame hurts your brain.
I had to learn to love you over and over again.
Thanks for your patience with me.
Be well, dear heart.

Yellow

The wall color of my bedroom in 1968
Special because I chose it myself
It was a happy color, still is for me

My daughter's blonde toddler curls
Bouncing as she laughed and ran
I'd give anything to witness that again

The color of the bruises on my fathers chest
As he healed from surgery at my home
I was pregnant, and he was drinking...but still

The color in my aunt's eyes
weeks before she passed
She gifted us with her humor anyway

The sun porch in our down sized house
2 rockers under a fan
If it is not my husband's cup of tea, that needs to be OK
with me

Between the (Phone) Lines

How are you doing? *(I'm worried about you)*

                        Fine *(but clearly I'm not)*

Beautiful day here *(Too far from you)*

          Really nice here (*stifling, almost unbearable*)

Any plans for the day? *(Trying to assess whether you feel like chatting or not)*

  Just meeting a friend for coffee, walking the dog *(I'm so not wanting to have this conversation, why did I answer)*

Well I won't keep you, just wanted to say I miss you *(Don't sound stressed, that will stress her)*

   I miss you too *(I really miss you, it just isn't the right time/space to share my emotional life with you now)*

Let's talk soon, love you!! *(Don't sound lonely, she might then feel anxious, or guilty, but she did say not to worry about that, but then again I too often say something that triggers her and I don't want to do that.)*

Love you too *(I really do, and I know you know that)*

Feminine Things

*Tune: My Favorite Things from
The Sound Of Music*

Cramping and bleeding, and hormonal raging
Sweating and farting that comes with our aging
Women have much more to deal with than men
We handle it all the best that we can!

Supplements, vitamins, why do we bother
It's never enough, there's always another
Every time we check our dumb Meta feed
There's an ad there to tell us what we need

Bras made for seniors, when we no longer want one
New underwear that accentuates our bum
Self care is big now but where do we start
Just finding the car in the lot is an art

Smooth the wrinkles,
Prevent hair loss,
There is no ending
We laugh about what we are targeted with
And then we don't feel - so bad!

Guide to Me: The Master Class

Wish I had known all of these myself 50 years ago

My air plants have died, please don't buy me living things, I can't handle more responsibility
Picking up vs cleaning, learn the difference
I tend to adopt the mood of those around me - optimism and humor are favorites
I suffer from a condition called Misophonia - intolerance of loud chewing (especially gum), finger drumming...
Car trip secret - if I know you'll stop at any point so I can pee, I probably won't need to
Tears, crying - this happens often; when it does, let's please keep talking unless I ask to stop
Silence - I love it because in my head I'm never not having a conversation, reviewing a conversation or singing
If I say I burned the roast, even if you don't smell anything, it means I'd like us to go out for dinner
Friends - I need time with my cohort of ladies to recharge, to exchange stories and ideas with my own

kind

Foods - there are some I Don't Like, never have, and approaching age 70, might never

Sleep - I apparently need 8+ hours of sleep in order to feel human. Much less than that I don't even get along with myself

Addiction to Zillow - I can't help it, I have had this addiction since childhood. I look at real estate listings compulsively

I believe some conversations would go better if people spoke with southern accents

I hate being in crowds, with their noise and proximity and exhaling and sneezing

I try to avoid having used air breathed toward my face

..........I really do sound like a bitch

Shopping - my best exercise, best therapy, best financial management training. I don't spend a ton, love thrifting, but some retail therapy seems to be required. If I buy one thing I promise myself to get rid of two!

Don't ask me to relax, that will never ever help me to relax

I loath being tickled. Now that I've said that I will feel betrayed and angry if you ever tickle me

I don't like surprises unless I plan them

I aim to not ask for help so if I need to ask more than once I'll likely just try to do it myself

Requesting that I make pasta because you're hungry for

it is one example of a big deposit in my emotional bank
account
I dislike rushing now. I've learned to slow down and
apparently I like it (you might be reading this as you
wait in the car)
Doing nothing is becoming quite appealing, and going
forward it'll be referred to as "basking in the present"
I will take responsibility for my own orgasms but I love
and appreciate a man who cares about them
I still adore list-making, but not quite as much as I used
to. I'm much more accepting of procrastination
I like to play music loudly and sing when I'm either
alone, or when I'm wearing my hearing aids (which you
will notice)
I need occasional time alone at home in order to
rejuvenate and reset
I love to dance, even when I'm by myself
I enjoy socializing but will suddenly just be done - then
I'd like to go home and let the world be quiet
Once I brush my teeth at bed time it's too late to bring
up controversial topics or important conversations
I like clothes and a good hair day, they can impact my
mood - not proud of that, but there it is
I can't imagine ever being too full for a morning bun, a
turtle sundae or Rice Krispies treats, just in case you ever
wonder

It is obviously never too late to learn more about how much my childhood explains who I am today - just wow ....

Apology

Dear Alice,

You may recall (that's not to imply that your memory isn't sharp, just that meeting us might not have been important enough for you to intentionally remember) that about 12 years ago you and your husband met my husband and me for dinner at Georgio's to share your experience and perhaps offer advice about having a son diagnosed with Schizophrenia.

My son had just been diagnosed and we were hungry to hear survival stories. I recall that your smile seemed worn, like a sweater that hung in your closet for years and you had grabbed as you left the house as an extra layer just in case. I sensed pity in your eyes and I felt myself wanting to impress you with the hope and energy I was bringing to our family's new reality. My son had been hospitalized only once (one and done I imagined) and was accepting medication at the time. He was still recognizable as the son I raised and I had faith that this disease was something he could learn to manage and then move on to live a happy life.

You talked about the many "typical" milestones your son had already missed and how heartbreaking it was when

his friends graduated, got married, welcomed babies. I
didn't want to end up as inconsolable as you seemed.
Your husband seemed to take a more practical approach
to the journey, or was perhaps just a better actor than
you. I am so sorry I saw you then as such a permanently
wounded mother. As if that was a choice you made that I
would certainly avoid.

I was asked the other day how long I grieved the loss of
the life I envisioned for my boy and more importantly
the life he would have created for himself. I believe my
watery eyes held a similar weary, preoccupied gaze as I
explained that the grief never ends, that I eventually
learned to walk alongside it. I am sincerely sorry, Alice.
If you ever want to get a cup of tea with me and share
how you feel, please don't hesitate to respond. I will hear
you this time.

wait...Wait....WAIT!

So many words crowd the tip of my tongue
They fall off and leave a trail behind me
I drag them along in case I need them later
I don't tell anyone it is the reason I'm walking more
slowly
Preoccupation instantly converts ten minutes to an hour
It's already 1? Today is Tuesday? Wait, WAIT, is this the
night we....no, no, never mind
I don't think Sudoku or Wordle can fix this, but it's worth
a try
Husband, I hope that if we each forget the other
Our love affair will begin again and again and again

Buster

Blessed to be retired but not too tired
I greatly anticipated your birth
During that 2020 Covid summer
Savoring regular updates from Arizona about the
pregnancy
Welcoming you to your forever home was a frequent
bedtime fantasy
when the news was too dour to metabolize
Amazon drivers dropped packages and grabbed a snack
from the sustenance bin outside our door
I prepared the nursery, as devoted to nesting as any
1950's housewife
My book club threw a puppy shower for me, any excuse
for a celebration from six feet away
I saved hundreds of videos in my YouTube library so I
could train you, groom your hair, and finally be a perfect
mommy
Daddy picked you up and delivered you to me in
Wisconsin that September
A fuzzy bundle of black and white - we were smitten
new parents
I scheduled vet appointments and puppy socialization
classes
I got up in the night if you cried (or woke daddy to check

on you)
Four years later, you are a smart, adorable canine who
identifies as a human who accepts that he's never had
sex
You have a younger sister - a rescue, to proudly offset
that you are indeed a designer sheepadoodle (and about
which we felt a tad sheepish)
You loudly announce mail delivery, passing school
children and invited guests
I have thousands of photos of you with your adoring
daddy
You never sass back, interrupt me or roll your eyes when
I am completely confident I know what is best for you
Your head tilts side to side as you try to comprehend
every word I say, no one in my life more attentive
Your mahogany brown eyes lock into mine - pure love,
total devotion
You never divulge if I nap on the sofa, eat cookies for
lunch or cannot get out of bed
You will never betray me when I lie and say I feel fine or
I have no pain
You burrow next to me and become my furnace when
this body will not warm itself
With deepest gratitude I trust you will keep your
promise
And take care of daddy
When only you can see that I am still here

After Life

When the energy of me changes
And I am free of this human form
I will still be here beside you
But no more will I feel worn

I will try to help you see that
Any worries you have got
Even the ones that hold you down
In the end will matter not

So please be kind to each other
For kindness is blessing itself
You will never be able to give love
If you can not love yourself

I believe only in angels
Who live among us and give
Those of who need reminders
That we need each other to live

After I no longer occupy space
It will not mean I am gone
The stories you recall and share
Keep me in your heart and strong

For energy can never be
Created or destroyed
This is scientific law
A truth we can not void

It helps me when I miss my folks
To know they are still with me
And when you share your memories
That is where I will be